wedish Proverbs

"Fair flowers don't remain long by the wayside."

Collected by Joanne Asala

For Bill Orejudos. "It is never too far to a friend's house."

Acknowledgments

A special thank-you to Tom Blanck, St. Paul, Minnesota, for use of his historic collection of Swedish books; Dr. John Lofgren, former director of the American Swedish Institute in Minneapolis, Minnesota, for assistance with the manuscript; Kerstin Olsson Van Gilder, Mary Lou Hattery, and Dean and Charlotte Anderson. Editorial Staff: Dorothy Crum and John Zug. Design: Robyn B. Loughran.

Front Cover: Baltic Islands near Stockholm. Back Cover: Midsummer Church-boat in Dalarna. Photographs ©1994 Joan Liffring-Zug. Illustrations in this book are from *Svenska Turist-Föreningens Årsskrift* by Ezaline Boheman. Published by Wahlström and Widstrand. Stockholm, 1906 and 1913.

Select List of Consulted Sources and Recommended Reading

Arnfeldt, Arvid. *Winged Words*. Stockholm, ca. 1890.
Bechtel, John H. *Proverbs, Maxims and Phrases Drawn from Many Lands*. London, 1906.
Christy, Robert. *Proverbs Maxims and Phrases*. New York, 1887.
Conklin, George. *The World's Best Proverbs*. Philadelphia, 1906.
Dennys, E.M. *Proverbs and Quotations of Many Lands*. London, 1890.
Hood, E.P. *The World of Proverb and Parable*. London, 1885.
Hulme, F. Edward. *Proverb Lore*. London: Elliot Stock, 1902.
Johnson, H. *Proverbs*. New York, 1885.
Kelly, Walter K. *Proverbs of All Nations*. London, 1859.
Kelly, Walter K. *A Collection of the Proverbs of All Nations*. Andover, 1879.
King, W. F. H. *Classical and Foreign Quotations*. London, 1889.
Marvin, D. E. *Curiosities in Proverbs*. London, 1916.
Mayo. *Stories and Sayings of Europe*. London, 1912.
Middlemore, James. *Proverbs, Sayings and Comparisons in Various Languages*. London, 1889.
O'Leary, C.F. *The World's Best Proverbs and Proverbial Phrases*. St. Louis, 1907.
Renterdahl, H. *Old Proverbs from the Swedish*. 1840.
Renterdahl, H. *Swedish Book of Proverbs*. 1865.
Shearer, William. *Wisdom of the World in Proverbs*. New York, 1904.

The Penfield Press Proverb Series

$10.95 each; shipping $4.95. Prices subject to change.
Swedish Proverbs (this book)   Scandinavian Proverbs
Danish Proverbs   Finnish Proverbs
Norwegian Proverbs   Words of Wisdom from the Vikings
For a complete catalog of titles send $2.00 to:
Distributed by Penfield Books, 215 Brown Street, Iowa City, Iowa 52245
Copyright ©1994 Joanne Asala
ISBN: 0941016-98-6   Library of Congress #94-065663

Table of Contents

·VÄTTERN · I · MORGONSTÄMNING·

𝕵ntroduction

If you want to know a people, study their proverbs. Sweden's rich literary heritage is full of homespun philosophy, simple truths, bits of collective wisdom, and good old common sense. Scholars define a proverb as "a short, wise saying used for a long time by many people." The Swedes put it another way, "a proverb says what all men think."

The Swedish people love beauty, and even their most practical, everyday items are works of art. So, too, are their proverbs. I was delighted to rediscover many of the same words of wisdom that were spoken by my great-grandparents, immigrants from the western regions of Finland.

So enjoy these short, pithy statements from a centuries-old culture, and perhaps you will find that the wisdom of our ancestors still speaks to us today.

About the Author
Joanne Asala is the owner of Kalevala Books, a company that publishes folklore and fairy tale collections. Of Finnish and Polish descent, she grew up in Bloomingdale, Illinois, a suburb of Chicago, and graduated from the University of Iowa, where she studied medieval literature and languages.

Joanne has collaborated with her cousin, Jason Asala, on a children's version of the Middle English ballad *Sir Gawain and the Green Knight*, and has edited a collection of Celtic folktales called *Whistling Jigs to the Moon: Tales of Irish and Scottish Pipers*. Her titles for Penfield Press include *Norwegian Proverbs*, *Polish Proverbs*, *Words of Wisdom from the Vikings*, *Fairy Tales of the Slav Peasants and Herdsmen*, and *Trolls Remembering Norway*—a compilation of stories and essays of trolls in the United States and Norway. She is the editor of several collections of student poetry, including *The Ugly Caterpillar* and *Shadows in the Snow*.

Love and Marriage

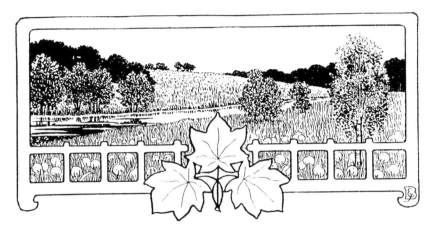

Love is a dew that falls
on both nettles
and lilies.

Midsummer night is not long, but
it sets many cradles rocking.

A life without love is like a year
without summer.

A man is often
    too young for marriage,
    but a man is never
        too old to love.

He who cannot
kindle a fire
cannot love.

No thief steals love,
    but love often makes thieves.

Wedlock is like an eel basket.
    Those who are out want to
    get in, and those who are in
    want to get out.

It is well to seek a wife in the
    village, but not in the street.

No one can live on beauty, but
    one can die for it.

Love often creeps where it
    should not grow.

Love has made heroes of many
    and fools of many more.

Love is a flower
    which at marriage
        bears fruit.

The married man has many cares,
    the bachelor many more.

A man without a wife is like a
man without conviction.

A man without a wife is
a man without thought.

Bachelors grow foolish.

Beauty without virtue
is like a rose
without scent.

Wisdom and Folly

We all have a fool
    beneath our clothes,
    but some hide it
        better than others.

Empty barrels
    make the loudest rattle.

One gains wisdom
        through suffering.

Unnecessary wisdom is
    twofold foolishness.

One finds many
gray hairs but
few wise men.

A wise man has his tongue
    in his heart.

It is better to be a fool
    than to make
    another person
            feel foolish.

The wise man is
        only cheated once.

Wisdom without use is like
fire without warmth.

If a fool could
keep silent,
he would not
be a fool.

Philosophy and Religion

A quiet word stills anger.

Trust in God makes
        the nation strong.

Blessed is he
    who knows how
            to forgive.

The rope has never been made
that can bind thought.

A clear conscience is
the best pillow.

In calm seas
every ship has a
good captain.

All beginnings are difficult.

Praise counsel when you have
heeded it, and ale when
you have drunk it.

The rich man rides and
the poor man goes on foot,
but both reach
Judgment Day
equally fast.

STORA · PORJUSFALLEN · RLD ·

The greater
the need,
the nearer
the Lord is.

Everyone has
his own devil,
and some have two.

In a little house
the Lord has a corner,
in a big house
He stands in the hall.

Dust is still dust, no matter
how near to Heaven
it is blown.

One is either
a friend of our Lord
or an enemy.

Man seeks to reach the Lord,
gold seeks to reach the soul.

When our Lord gives,
one should keep
the sack open.

The Lord often
goes about in
worn-down shoes.

The Lord gives
   every bird its food,
but He does not
   cast it into the nest.

own
on the Farm

FÄBODVALLAR VID TÄNNSJÖN

Don't throw away
        the old bucket
    until you know whether
        the new one
        will hold water.

A lazy man raises poor cabbage.

He who cannot carry the stone
    must roll it.

Not all Autumns fill granaries.

When can a lazy man work?
    In Fall there is
        too much mud.
    In Spring there is
        too much water.
    In Winter
        the cold is biting.
    In Summer
        the heat burns.

The work praises the man.

In Spring the
    farmer carries
    a bag of ignorance,
in Autumn
    a bag of wisdom.

By doing nothing
        we learn to do ill.

The clock must be
        master of the house.

A short man gets a strawberry
        from the earth quicker than
        a tall man a star from
        the heavens.

Weeds grow best
        in good soil.

New brooms sweep best.

A good pig
   will find its way
      home at night.

The little pigs
      would grunt in fear
   if they knew the suffering
      of the boar.

Even a blind hen
   will sometimes
      find a grain.

Everyone jumps
   over a low fence.

TALLBEVUXEN · SANDÅS ·

If one sheep bleats,
the whole barnyard
is thirsty.

Give the servant
good food and
the cows will
yield more milk
and the cat will
drink less.

Nature, Day and Night

Even the smallest
of stars shines
in the darkness.

Don't believe the tears
of the ocean, for its eyes
are always full of water.

Day gives
            and night takes.

No one is
      too poor
            to help another,
      and no one is
      too rich never
            to need help.

What the waterfall brings,
      the stream takes away.

A tall tree bends,
      but it does not break.

Water goes where
            water has been.

There is no night so long
    that a day
        will not follow it.

A rotting tree leans
    long before it falls.

One who mocks a stream
    should stand by the sea.

One bird in the hand is better
        than two on the roof.

He who has taken
    the bear into the boat
    must cross over with him.

The afternoon knows
    what the morning
        never dreamed.

He on whom the sun shines
    asks not about the moon.

One good day often costs a
    hundred bad nights.

The evening is
    the crown of
        the day.

The light shines for others and
    not for itself.

The day we fear
    hurries toward us,
        the day we long for creeps.

That which is
    to become a nettle
        must learn
            to sting early.

A narrow river
is soon rowed,
a shallow ocean
measured,
a small mind
stirred.

Truth and Lies

PARTUR AF SVINORA SJÓFALLET

If lies were as heavy
as stones to carry,
many would speak
only the truth.

Mistakes of others
make no law.

The greatest right is often
the greatest wrong.

Better to suffer
for the truth
than be praised
for the lie.

Eat only
what is ripe,
speak only
what is true.

If every lie were to
knock out a tooth,
there would be many
toothless people.

The Change of Seasons

What is hidden
in snow
comes forth
in the thaw.

One swallow does not
    make Summer.

No one thinks of the snow
    that fell last year.

Warm days
    in Winter
        are still cold.
Cold days
    in Summer
        are still warm.

The Winter
        does not pass
    without looking
                behind.

He who lies idle
　　　when the wind is mild,
　　must row when the wind
　　　blows against him.

Earth in Spring
is worth more
than grass
in Autumn.

istoric Proverbs

It will not do to go
berry-picking with
the nobleman;
he will keep both berries
and baskets.

When the cat is away,
the rats will dance
on the table.

VADSTENA · SLOTT · FRÅN · LANDSIDAN ·

Lords without virtue
are like lanterns
without light.

Money travels along
the high road.

In war it is better to
fasten one's horse
to someone else's manger.

What is gained in war
is eaten in war.

Better coarse cloth
        than bare thighs.

He who would
        harvest honey
must endure the
        sting of the bees.

A piece of bread in one's pocket
        is better than a
        feather in one's hat.

Neither hat nor crown
    ever held up
        against a
            headache.

He who eats his bread
in solitude,
saddles his horse
alone.

The mill goes
with the current
and the old woman
against it.

When the cat
and mouse agree,
the farmer's in trouble.

A poor woman has
many troubles:
crying babies, wet firewood,
leaking kettle, and
a grumpy husband.

· LAPSK · TORFKÅTA · VID · HÄLINGEN ·

In war
all suffer defeat,
even victors.

War makes thieves
and peace hangs them.

The rooster often crows
without a victory.

A man is needed for a day,
a dog for a week,
and a woman always.

riends and Neighbors

No one has
so big a house
that he does not need
a good neighbor.

When two do the same,
it is not always the same.

Everyone's friend
is often
everyone's fool.

The house that is built
with every man's advice
rarely gets a roof.

He who has
a little money has
a lot of friends.

One should go invited to
a friend's house
in good fortune,
and uninvited
in misfortune.

The comforter's head
          never aches.

Guests should not forget
     to go home.

No one has peace
     longer than
          his neighbor wishes.

It is never too far
     to a friend's house.

One must learn to
     make others happy
if one wants
     to be happy.

GÅRDAR · I · LEKSANDS · SOCKEN

We should remember
to think well
and speak well
of one another.

Exchange of gifts
makes friendship
last.

ome and Family

FINNSTUGAN · VID · SVÅNGEA

Being away
is fine,
being home
is best.

The child acts
in the village
as he has learned
at home.

Late to church,
early to the mill,
this is the way
one returns home sooner.

The pine cone does not fall
far from the tree.

Do not brag of
your father's reputation,
what you have is your own.

Water is thinner than blood.

The child puts finery
        in her mouth,
the young woman puts it on,
and the old woman keeps it
        in her wooden chest.

Honor the house in
        which you were born,
the tree that
        gave you shade,
and the village where
        you were raised.

All little girls are good,
so where do the
naughty old women
come from?

A woman's heart
sees more than
ten men's eyes.

The stony earth
grows the corn,
but the woman
does the work.

Remain a child so that
your children may
always love you.

Small children, small worries;
big children, big worries.

A child is
a certain worry and
an uncertain joy.

The motherless child
is in the way when
the stepmother bakes.

Food and Drink

· STRÅKENS · NORDLIGASTE · ÄNDE ·

The sweetest wine
   makes the
        sharpest vinegar.

Eaten bread
   is soon forgotten.

He who has burnt himself once
   blows on his soup.

Hunger is the
best seasoning.

One cannot
make soup
out of beauty.

Do not cross the river
to find water.

That which is eaten
from the pot
never comes to
the platter.

The stomach teaches
the hunter to shoot.

When the stomach is satisfied,
the food is bitter.

Every cake
seeks its match.

Where wine
goes in,
wit goes out.

ural Wisdom

TOLLTORPS BRO · NISNARE KANAL ·

The rich
      have money,
the poor
      have children.

If you want the kernel
    you must crush the nut.

Many mouths make
an empty dish.

The world's reward
is ingratitude.

The rich man has five senses,
the poor man has six.

The poor are not
those who
have little,
but those who
need much.

Poverty does not
abide stealing,
and wealth does not
forbid it.

·KUNGSHALL·KARLSKRONA·

Don't shout before
        you are across
                the stream.

To read and
        not know
    is to plow
        and not sow.

Good will draws
        the load to the village.

A wound never
      heals enough
            to hide a scar.

He is not rich
   who has not
      anything old.

Hope keeps the poor alive.
    Fear often kills the rich.

Better to bow
      than hit your head
   on the door lintel.

outh and Old Age

With a young lawyer,
    you lose your inheritance,
   with a young doctor
    you lose your health.

Take hold of grace,
   for younger
    you will never be.

As the young sing,
              so the old chirp.

The young do not know
              what age is,
and the old forget
              what youth was.

Age does not
      grant wisdom,
      it only makes one
           go more slowly.

Being young
      is a fault which
           improves daily.

The mind of
   the young is
      like water in
         a bucket,
   it splashes out
      from all sides.

Age's virtues are
   dearly purchased.

The young man shows
   what the old man was.

He who does not
commit follies
in youth
commits them
in old age.

Life and Death

He who fears death
has lost his zest for life.

Better a good death than an evil life.

What life gives,
       death takes.

Death is
      the final doctor.

He who did not
escape from birth
cannot escape
from death.

Death helps us out
          of difficulties,
      but the price is high.

There is no medicine
        against death.

Death is
        the Lord's broom.

Advice
should not be
viewed from in front,
but from behind.

BEN'S ROBOT

ROBIN STEVENSON
Illustrated by DAVID PARKINS

ORCA BOOK PUBLISHERS

Library and Archives Canada Cataloguing in Publication

Stevenson, Robin, 1968-
Ben's robot / written by Robin Stevenson ; illustrated by David Parkins.

(Orca echoes)
ISBN 978-1-55469-153-1

I. Parkins, David II. Title. III. Series: Orca echoes

PS8637.T487B45 2010   jC813'.6   C2009-906871-0

First published in the United States, 2010
Library of Congress Control Number: 2009940933

Summary: Ben discovers having a bossy friend isn't that much fun,
even if it is a real walking, talking robot.

Orca Book Publishers gratefully acknowledges the support for its publishing programs provided
by the following agencies: the Government of Canada through the Canada Book Fund and the
Canada Council for the Arts, and the Province of British Columbia
through the BC Arts Council and the Book Publishing Tax Credit.

Mixed Sources
Product group from well-managed forests,
controlled sources and recycled wood or fiber
www.fsc.org Cert no. SW-COC-000952
© 1996 Forest Stewardship Council
FSC

*Orca Book Publishers is dedicated to preserving the environment and has printed this book
on paper certified by the Forest Stewardship Council.*

Typesetting by Teresa Bubela
Cover artwork and interior illustrations by David Parkins
Author photo by David Lowes

Orca Book Publishers   Orca Book Publishers
PO Box 5626, Stn. B   PO Box 468
Victoria, BC Canada   Custer, WA USA
V8R 6S4   98240-0468

www.orcabook.com
Printed and bound in Canada.

13 12 11 10 • 4 3 2 1

For my amazing son, Kai.
I love you forever and for always.

Chapter One

Ben stood up straight. He stuck his arms out in front of him. They were as stiff and rigid as two metal poles. "I'm a robot," he said. It didn't sound quite right, so he said it again. This time his voice was flat. "I. Am. A. Robot."

Jessy grinned at him. She pulled a piece of cardboard out of her pocket. She held it out in her hand. "I brought my remote control," she told him. "Robot, go forward!" She pretended to push a button.

Ben took a few steps, keeping his legs straight. He imagined his knee joints were held together with steel bolts. Stride, *squeak*. Stride, *squeak*. He stopped. "My hinges need oil," he said in his robot voice.

Jessy giggled. She ran over and pretended to squirt oil into his knee joints. "There you go, Robot. Is that better?"

"Knee joints. Check." Ben took a few more steps. The squeak was gone. "Elbow joints. Check." He lifted his arms and dropped them again. "Check complete."

Jessy sat down on the damp grass. She pulled her shiny black hair into a ponytail. "Now what?"

"What do you mean?" Ben asked. They played this game every day at recess. Jessy should know what came next. "We still have to complete the checks. You know. Circuit boards, batteries, sensors." He switched back to his robot voice. "Please give your next command."

"Penny and Finn are playing in the sandbox," Jessy said. She pointed at the school playground. "Want to go join them? Finn brought his dinosaurs. They're burying them and digging them up."

"Sand could damage my circuits," Ben said.

2

"Just drop the robot voice and talk to me for a minute." Jessy shook her head. Her ponytail swung from side to side. "Come on, Ben. It would be fun."

"I cannot. Sand could damage—"

Jessy cut him off. "Yeah, yeah. Your circuits. I know." She stood up and brushed grass off her jeans. "Look. The sand is still wet from the rain last night. Penny and Finn are making a volcano."

"Water could make me rust," Ben said. He felt worried. Why wasn't Jessy just playing their game like she did every day? Last year, when they were in first grade, they had played Dinosaurs, and then Pirates. This year it was Robots. He had liked all their games, but Robots was the best. Ben loved robots more than anything.

"I'm bored," Jessy said.

"Check circuits. Check batteries." Ben tried to keep his voice flat. Robots didn't get worried. They just did their jobs.

Jessy sighed. "How come you're always giving me the orders? I'm supposed to be the one in charge." She held up her remote control. "Shouldn't I be telling *you* what to do?"

Ben started to shrug. Then he stopped himself. Robots didn't shrug. "Please give your next command," he said.

Jessy pointed her remote control at him. "Quit being a robot," she said, pretending to push a button. "Come and play in the sandbox."

Ben stared at her. He didn't want to stop being a robot. "I am Robot KX 749," he said. "Robots do not play."

"Well, I'm going to," Jessy said. She threw her remote control on the ground. "This is a dumb game, Ben. We just do the same stuff all the time, and it's boring." She ran off to join Penny and Finn.

Ben watched her go. Jessy stepped into the sandbox and sat down beside Penny and Finn.

Ben's arms and legs felt heavy and stiff, as if they really were made of metal. His eyes stung and his throat hurt. For a second, he thought he might cry. *You can't,* he told himself. *Robots don't cry.* He sniffed a couple of times. Then he looked at Jessy's remote control lying on the grass. She had left it behind as if it was garbage. Ben picked it up and slipped it into his back pocket.

Chapter Two

Jessy had a karate class after school. So Ben had to walk home by himself. Most days he liked walking with Jessy. Today he was glad to be on his own. He was still mad about what had happened at lunchtime.

Besides, on the way home they always collected robot parts for Ben's collection. What if Jessy didn't want to do that anymore either? Jessy had been his best friend for as long as he could remember. He couldn't imagine what he would do if she started spending recess with Penny and Finn instead of him. Maybe he would stay home and not go to school at all. That would show Jessy.

This was the first year Ben had been allowed to walk home by himself. It was only a few blocks. He had to cut through the school playground and turn left down a quiet street. Then, before he turned onto his street, there was the best thing ever. The Dumpster.

Real garbage got tossed inside the Dumpster, out of sight. Ben didn't care about what was inside the Dumpster. The good part was the piles of stuff left beside the Dumpster—stuff people didn't want anymore but thought someone else might. Sometimes the stuff was in boxes with the word *FREE* written on them in fat black marker.

Ben and Jessy had found all kinds of amazing things beside the Dumpster. Jessy wasn't allowed to take home the stuff she found. Her parents didn't like things that came from secondhand stores, let alone from free piles. So Ben got to keep it all. And what treasures he had found! Some of his best finds were an old toy pinball game with only the tiniest of cracks, a perfectly good race car, a book about bridges, a wooden steam engine with a broken axle, a boxed set of three opera music CDs and about a million spare parts for the robot he was building.

Ben kicked a pinecone along in front of him as he walked through the playground. Fall leaves crunched under his feet. Today had been a lousy day. His stomach felt squirmy every time he thought about it. Stupid Jessy. But as the giant green Dumpster came into view, he started to feel better. Maybe today there would be a new free pile, one with something really great in it. He hoped to find another race car or a Tonka truck. Or, best of all, some new parts for the robot he was building. Then Jessy would be sorry she had gone to karate and missed out on the discovery.

Ben ran over to the Dumpster. Sure enough, there was a new cardboard box beside it. A piece of paper taped to the box said *HELP YOURSELF*. He dropped to his knees and looked inside.

9

Clothes. Boring. He pulled those out and piled them on the grass. Kitchen stuff. Not a good sign. Boxes that had chipped mugs and old frying pans almost never had anything good in them. Still, you never knew. He lifted a plastic cutting board. Beneath it, he saw something so exciting, so wonderful and so perfect his heart skipped a beat.

He took a small green square, no bigger than his hand, out of the box. The square was covered with wires and knobs and dials. A circuit board! It was the exact part he needed to complete his robot.

Chapter Three

Ben's mom was raking leaves on the front lawn when he arrived home.

"Oh no," she said when she saw him. "Oh no. Not more junk, Ben."

"Mom! Look. It's perfect." He held out his find.

His mom put down her rake and bent closer. "What is it?"

"A circuit board," Ben said.

"Well, I can see that. I mean, what is it for? Why do you need a broken old circuit board?"

Ben shook his head. He had explained this so many times, but his mom never quite understood. "For building stuff, Mom. You know."

"More inventions? What is it now?" she asked.

Ben dropped his voice to a whisper. "Don't tell anyone."

She pretended to zip her lips shut. "Not a word, I promise."

"Do you want to see?" Ben pointed to the shed. "I'll show you."

Ben's mom followed him over to the shed. She stood back while Ben pushed the door open. "There," he said.

The walls of the shed were piled high with his beautiful junk. There were metal pipes, spools of wire, wooden blocks, a giant roll of tinfoil, and boxes overflowing with springs, screws, nuts and bolts. It looked like a mess, but Ben knew exactly where to find everything. He had built wind generators and pinball machines and solar-powered marble launchers. And now, right in the middle of it all, propped up against an empty wooden crate, sat Ben's current project, Robot KX 749.

"Wow." His mom's eyes widened. "Is that...um..."

Ben jumped up and down. "Yes! It's a robot." He looked at KX 749 and couldn't stop grinning. The robot's head was a shiny metal bowl with plastic googly eyes glued on. A straight red wire formed his mouth and gave him a grumpy expression. His arms and legs were made from slim steel pipes bound together with wire. His body was a block of wood. On the front of the block, Ben had drawn a rectangle.

"See, Mom? The circuit board will fit here perfectly." He held it up to the robot's chest. Sure enough, it was exactly the right size. He could hardly wait to glue it in place.

"It's wonderful," his mom told him. She looked around the shed again. "Boy. You're something else, kiddo."

Ben frowned. "Something else?"

She laughed. "It means I think you're great. And it also means you have enough beautiful junk," she said. "No more, okay? Soon you won't be able to fit in here yourself."

Ben laughed too. His mom often said he had too much junk, but he knew she didn't mean it. She always bought him pants with lots of pockets, so he could collect stuff. Besides, the things in his shed weren't really junk. Who wouldn't want to keep treasures like these?

Chapter Four

Ben had to do his homework and eat dinner before he was allowed to work on his robot. Dinner was bread, cheese, salad and fruit. Ben ate his bread frozen. He didn't like to eat anything cooked. His little sister Stella ate mush.

Stella sat in her high chair and banged a spoon on her tray. Mashed squash flew everywhere. One big orange glob landed right on Ben's arm.

"Mom!" he yelled. "Look what Stella did."

His mom tossed him a cloth. She kept chopping vegetables for the salad. Ben wiped the glob off his arm and glared at Stella. This was not a good day. "You're a slob," he told her. "Little pea brain."

"Ben…" His mom turned and frowned at him. "Be nice."

"She doesn't understand anyway." Stella had just turned one and a half. Her hair stood straight up, as fine and pale as dandelion fluff. She didn't talk yet.

"She does so understand," said his mom. "Anyway, even if she didn't, you still shouldn't be rude to her." She carried the salad to the table. "Did you have a bad day?"

Ben thought about Jessy. He didn't want to talk about it, so he shrugged. "It was okay," he said. Ben took a bite of frozen bread and picked a few slices of red pepper out of the salad. He didn't like green vegetables. He only ate yellow and red ones. "Can I go work on my robot?"

"That's all you're eating?" his mom asked.

Stella tossed another glob of mush in his direction. Then she picked up her bowl and dumped it on the floor.

"I'm not hungry," Ben said.

"Oh, Stella." His mom wiped flecks of squash off her jeans. "Yes, okay. Off you go. And if that robot can clean floors or fix dishwashers, send it in here."

Out in the shed, KX 749 sat waiting. The robot leaned against a wooden crate. Its steel-pipe legs stuck straight out. Its arms dangled at its sides.

"Hi, Robot," Ben whispered. In the dim light, the robot's googly eyes glinted. "Wait until I get this circuit board on you. You'll be perfect."

Ben twisted the lid off his glue bottle. He held the circuit board carefully in one hand. If Jessy were here, she would be so excited to see the robot finished. Or maybe she wouldn't even care, since she thought robots were boring. Ben couldn't understand how anyone could think that. "Stupid Jessy," he muttered to himself. He smeared glue evenly over the back of the circuit board. Then he pushed it onto the robot's chest. "Here you go, little robot. You're all done."

KX 749 looked perfect. Ben grinned widely. If only Jessy were here, this would be the best day ever.

And then something happened that made Ben forget all about Jessy.

KX 749's googly eyes moved from side to side. They moved up and down. Its steel-pipe legs gave a little kick. Its red wire mouth began to move. And in a flat robotic voice, it began to speak.

Chapter Five

"I. Am. Robot. K. X. 7. 4. 9," Ben's robot said.

Ben stared at it.

"I am Robot KX 749," the robot said again. "Please respond."

"Um..." Ben couldn't think what to say. "Are you, are you a real robot? Alive, I mean?"

"Robots are not alive," the robot said.

"Sorry. I just meant, well, can you really talk?" Ben couldn't believe it. His wind generator hadn't really made wind. His solar-powered marble launcher had looked good, but it had never done anything. In fact, nothing he had ever built before had really worked. Not like this.

"It would seem so. Yes, I can talk." The robot didn't look very happy about it.

"Wow! This is so cool," said Ben. Wait until Jessy saw this. She wouldn't think robots were boring then.

"I do not know if it is cool," the robot said. "I have not been given any sensors. For all I know, I am overheating."

"I didn't mean cool as in cold," Ben said.

The robot interrupted him. "For all I know, my circuits are too hot or too cold. For all I know, I am freezing."

"No, no. Don't worry. You are fine. You are just right." Ben hoped this was true. The nights sometimes got quite cold. Perhaps he should bring the robot inside overnight. The rule was that his beautiful junk stayed in the shed. But maybe once his mom saw what had happened, she would let the robot stay in the house.

"Um…Robot? Can you clean floors?"

The robot's mouth turned down at the corners. "I am KX 749. My name is not Robot."

"Sorry, KX. Can I just call you KX for short?"

The robot rolled its googly eyes. "I suppose."

"So, KX, can you clean floors?"

"I have not been given hands. I cannot grip a mop. I cannot grip a broom." KX's voice was even flatter than usual.

Ben looked at the robot's arms. The steel pipes ended at the wrist. How could he have forgotten hands? "Sorry," he said again. "Maybe I can fix that." He picked the robot up. "I have to show you to my mom," he said. "She's going to be so amazed. Even if you can't clean floors."

Mom was changing Stella's diaper on the living-room floor. Ben wrinkled his nose. It smelled gross.

"Hi, Ben. Did you finish your robot?" his mom asked.

"Yeah. Mom, you're not going to believe this." Ben held up his robot. "Check this out."

She glanced up. "Ben! No junk in the house. You know the rule."

He stood the robot up, balanced on the ends of its steel-pipe legs. "Yeah, but, Mom, this isn't junk anymore. You won't believe what's happened."

The phone rang. Mom stood up. She had the dirty diaper in her hand. "Watch Stella for a minute, okay? I have to get that."

Ben sighed. He laid the robot down and sat on the floor beside Stella. She kicked her bare legs in the air and babbled away in her nonsense talk. He wished she would start talking properly. She had not yet spoken one single real word. His mom had taken her to see Dr. Ross. The doctor said Stella was doing fine, and all babies did things at their own pace. Ben figured Stella just didn't have much to say.

"See my robot, Stella?" he said. "Pretty cool, huh?"

"I do not know," the robot said. "I have not been given a sensor."

"Yeah, yeah," said Ben. He was getting tired of the robot's complaints. "Listen, you're lucky I made you at all, okay? If it wasn't for me, you wouldn't exist."

Stella pointed at the robot and started to laugh. "Ah wa ga bo," she said.

"Robot," Ben told her. "Say *robot*, Stella."

"Sorry," his mom said, coming back into the room. "That was the dishwasher repair guy."

Ben wondered if KX could fix a dishwasher. Probably not, with no hands. He picked it up and held it high to show his mom. "Look at my robot!"

Mom picked up Stella. "It looks great. Really great." She sat Stella on one hip. "I have to get the baby into her pj's."

"Did you even look?" Ben asked. He put the robot back down. "Come on, KX. Show her what you can do."

"Clean floors, I hope," his mom said, laughing. "Or do laundry. I could use a laundry robot."

Ben gave the robot a poke. But nothing happened. KX 749 lay on the floor like a pile of junk.

Chapter Six

Ben carried his robot up to his room. He sat it on the carpet, next to his bed. The robot was only a bunch of pipes and wires and a pair of glued-on googly eyes. Had it really talked to him? Maybe he had imagined the whole thing. If only Stella could talk. Then he could ask her if she had heard the robot speak too.

Ben put on his red rocket-ship pajamas. He sat on the edge of his bed. "KX?" he whispered. "Are you still a real robot?"

"Of course I am," the robot answered. It turned to look at Ben, squeaking loudly as it moved. "My hinges need oil."

"I'll say." Ben smiled. So he hadn't imagined the robot had spoken after all. "I'll do it tomorrow, okay?"

"Affirmative."

Ben frowned. "What?"

"It means yes."

"Huh." Ben tried it out. "Affirmative. That's cool."

"I do not know if it is cool. I do not—"

"I know, I know. Could you stop going on about heat sensors? I don't know how to make one. Anyway, cool just means great. It means no problem." Now Ben and the robot had taught each other a new word. He leaned closer. "We're going to be friends, aren't we? I've always wanted a robot friend."

The robot didn't answer. Ben looked at its red wire mouth. It made a straight grumpy line. He wished he had given the robot a smiley mouth instead. That was one thing he liked about Jessy—her smile was so wide it seemed to stretch from ear to ear. And she smiled a lot. In fact, whenever Ben thought of Jessy, he pictured her with a big smile on her face.

"How come you didn't say anything when my mom was there?" asked Ben. "I wanted her to see you move and talk."

"Sorry," the robot said. Its voice sounded stiffer than usual. "She was big."

"Well, duh. She's a grown-up."

"She called me junk," the robot said. Its wire mouth looked sad.

"Oh." Ben wondered if a robot's feelings could be hurt. Did robots even have feelings? "She didn't know you were real," he said quickly. "She thought you were just something I made."

"Junk is garbage," the robot said. "Junk is stuff no one wants."

Ben shook his head firmly. "No way," he said. "I want it. I want all kinds of beautiful junk. And I want you too, KX. So can we be friends?"

The robot's eyes turned to look at him. "Maybe," it said. "I have never had a friend. I might not be that kind of robot."

"Oh, being friends is easy," Ben said. Then he remembered his fight with Jessy. Maybe it wasn't always that easy after all. He pushed the thought away. He hoped his mom would let him take KX to school tomorrow. Jessy was going to be surprised when she saw he had a real robot friend.

Chapter Seven

"The robot has to stay at home," Mom told Ben at breakfast. "I have already bent the rules by letting you keep it in the house. I don't think your teacher would want a robot in the classroom."

"He probably would if he knew it was a real one," Ben said.

She laughed. "Here we go again." She stood up and ruffled Ben's hair with her hand. Then she poured herself another coffee. "I love your imagination, but aren't you getting carried away?"

Ever since he woke up, Ben had been trying to tell his mom KX could move and talk. It didn't seem to matter what he said. She wouldn't believe him.

"No," Ben said. "I don't think so."

She laughed. "You are so adorable."

Ben hated being called adorable. It was almost as bad as being called cute. No one called real robot mechanics cute.

"It's true," he said. "My robot is real." He poked KX's wooden tummy hard. Stupid robot. "I'm going to show it to Jessy tomorrow." Jessy always came over after school on Tuesdays.

"Good idea." His mom smiled. "Maybe you two can help me make some cookies too."

"Maybe," Ben said. But if his mom was there, KX wouldn't talk. And then Jessy wouldn't believe him either.

Ben left KX safely hidden under his bed. He didn't think the robot would go anywhere. Still, he closed his bedroom door just in case.

When he got to school, the first thing he did was look for Jessy. She was late. He worried that she wasn't coming. Just as the bell rang, he saw her ride up on her bike. Her dad was jogging beside her.

Ben ran over to the bike rack. "Jessy, guess what?"

Jessy waved goodbye to her dad and turned to lock up her bike. "What?" She took off her helmet and smiled at him.

"You know my robot I've been building?"

"Of course." Jessy looked interested.

"Well..." Ben looked around to make sure no one was listening. He spoke in a whisper. "I know this sounds crazy, but it really works."

"Cool."

Ben didn't think she quite understood. "I don't just mean it looks good. I mean..."

"Come on, you two," Mr. McLeod, their teacher, called them into the school. "You can catch up at recess. Right now, we've got a Viking ship to build."

37

Ben sighed as he walked up the stairs to his classroom. It was hard to be excited about building model boats with Popsicle sticks and glue when you had a real robot in your bedroom.

He liked the Viking boat project though. Building things always made Ben happy. While he worked, he hummed to himself. Jessy would be so amazed when she found out about his robot. Maybe he wouldn't tell her at recess after all. Maybe he'd wait until after school and show her instead.

Chapter Eight

"So what do you want to do?" Jessy asked at recess. "I guess you probably want to play robots?"

Ben put his hand in his back pocket and found Jessy's remote control. He handed it to her. "Okay."

Jessy took the remote control. "Robot, forward."

Ben took a couple of steps. Then he thought of something. He hadn't given KX any feet. He would have to fix that if he wanted the robot to walk.

"Are your hinges okay?" Jessy asked.

Ben thought about how KX complained about everything. "Yeah, fine," he said.

"Circuits? Batteries?"

"Yeah. They're okay too."

Jessy frowned. "How come you're not talking like a robot?"

Ben shrugged. He wasn't sure why, but he didn't feel like playing robot today. "Want to play in the sandbox?" he asked.

Jessy looked surprised. "You don't want to play robot?"

"Maybe we could be robots in the sandbox," Ben said. After all, he didn't *really* have to worry about sand in his circuits.

Jessy laughed. "Okay! Race you!"

They ran to the sandbox together. Ben's legs didn't feel stiff or heavy at all.

After school, Ben and Jessy walked to Ben's house. Jessy walked her bike along the sidewalk. Ben was so excited, he skipped the whole way. He didn't even want to stop at the Dumpster to look for free stuff. He couldn't wait to get home to show Jessy his real robot.

"Hello, you two," Ben's mom said. "Want to come in for a snack?"

Jessy started to say yes, but Ben grabbed her arm. "I have to show you something first. Come on."

When he got to his room, Ben peeked under his bed. The robot was right where Ben had left it. Ben grabbed the robot's legs, gently slid it out and sat it up.

Jessy gasped. "Wow! It looks great!"

"Yeah! And check this out, Jessy. The robot really works." Ben stood up and looked at his robot. "KX, say something."

But KX said nothing.

"Come on, KX! Show Jessy what you can do."

Jessy giggled.

Ben frowned at KX. "Come on. Please?"

"Let's go get a snack," Jessy said. "It smells like your mom has made cookies."

"Come on, KX," Ben said again. "Please, please, please. Just say one word. Move your legs. Anything."

KX stared straight ahead. Its googly eyes were blank and lifeless.

Jessy shuffled her feet. She took a step toward the door. "Cookies, Ben. Let's go."

"You don't believe me, do you?" Ben turned to face Jessy. "You think I'm making it up."

"Yeah, but it's okay to pretend, Ben. I don't mind pretending with you." She shrugged. "I just think we should have cookies first."

Ben folded his arms across his chest. "Fine," he said. "You go ahead. I have to fix my robot."

"Fine," Jessy said. "I guess you would rather play with your stupid robot than a real friend anyway." She turned and stomped out of the room.

Chapter Nine

Ben couldn't decide if he was mad at Jessy for not believing him or mad at KX for making him look like a liar. Maybe he was mad about both.

"You know, you're nothing but trouble," Ben said. "I wish I had never made you."

KX's googly eyes blinked.

"Sure. Now that it's just you and me, you stop pretending you can't do anything." Ben scowled. "Why wouldn't you talk to Jessy?"

"You did not ask me a question. I had nothing to say."

"Look…" Ben thought hard. "Would you let someone see you move? Just once? So I know I'm not making this all up?"

"Maybe," said KX.

"Maybe?"

"Maybe if you did one thing for me," the robot said.

Ben didn't trust the robot. "Like what?"

"Feet. Hands."

"That's two things," Ben said.

"It is four. I need a pair of each."

Ben narrowed his eyes. "So if I make you hands and feet, you will show someone else what you can do?"

"Affirmative."

"Deal." Ben looked in his closet. What could he use? An old pair of gloves might work for hands. He found a pair of mittens under a pile of jigsaw puzzles. He taped them onto the end of the robot's arms with his duct tape.

Now for feet. Ben lifted the lid of his toy box and looked inside. "Hmmm. This old pair of roller skates might work." He lined the roller skates up with the robot's pipe legs. "Looks good, KX," he said. "You are going to be fast."

He taped the skates to the robot's ankles. He was wrapping the tape around and around a second time when someone knocked at his door.

"Ben?"

"Yes?"

His mom stepped into the room. Stella was sitting on her hip. "Jessy is downstairs eating a snack by herself. What's going on, Ben?"

"I have to finish this," Ben said.

"Jessy's upset," his mom said. "When you have a friend over, you should play with her. She won't want to come over here if you ignore her."

"It's not my fault," Ben argued. "She wouldn't..." He was about to explain that Jessy would not believe him about his robot being real. Then he stopped. After all, his mom didn't believe him either.

Ben sighed. He put down the roll of tape and followed his mom downstairs. His mom put Stella in

47

her playpen in the living room. Then she took Ben's hand and led him into the kitchen.

Jessy was sitting at the table. She had a gingerbread man in her hand. She had already eaten its feet. Ben's mom nudged him. "Sorry," he mumbled.

"It's okay," Jessy said. Her eyes looked a bit red. Ben wondered if she had been crying. He felt bad, but it wasn't really his fault. If anything, it was that stupid robot's fault. He sat down beside her.

"Want to play something else?" he said.

Jessy nodded. She handed him a gingerbread man. "Ohhh...Ben, I've got a good idea!"

"What?"

She whispered as if she was telling him a secret. "Vikings."

Ben felt an excited flutter in his tummy. He pictured the Viking ship they were building at school. He imagined fierce Vikings in capes and fur and horned helmets.

"Yeah," he said. "We'll need costumes."

Jessy bit off her gingerbread man's head and chewed slowly. "Let's look in the costume trunk," she said.

Mom smiled. "I bet I could turn those construction hats into Viking helmets."

"With horns?" Ben asked.

"You bet," she said.

Just then there was a squeal from the living room. "I better check on Stella," Mom said.

Ben and Jessy trailed into the living room. Stella was standing in her playpen, banging on the edge with one hand. She pointed at the front door with the other.

"What is it, honey? Is someone at the door? I didn't hear anyone." Ben's mom crossed the room, opened the door and looked out. "There's no one there."

"Wo boh go," Stella said. "Wo boh go."

Mom sighed. "Honey, I really wish you would learn a few words."

But Ben was staring at her. "Stella. Stella, say that again."

Stella looked at him and smiled. "Wo boh go," she said. She pointed at the front door. "Ben wo boh go."

Mom gasped. "Ben! She said your name, did you hear that?"

But Ben had heard more than his name. *Wo boh go. Robot go. Ben's robot go.* He ran across the room, out the open door and onto the sidewalk.

Nothing.

He turned and raced up to his room.

But he was too late. KX 749 was gone.

Chapter Ten

Ben couldn't believe it. He ran back downstairs and stared out the front door. His mom was on the phone. She was calling all her friends to tell them Stella had talked. Jessy came and stood beside him. "What's wrong?" she asked.

"My robot's gone," Ben said. "I made it feet out of my old roller skates. And now it's gone."

Jessy's eyes got big. "You weren't just teasing me?"

"No, it really did come alive." Ben scowled. "It wasn't a very nice robot though. It complained about everything. And it tricked me too." He told Jessy about the deal he had made with the robot. "I wanted you to see it move and talk."

Jessy looked thoughtful. "I guess it didn't really break the bargain," she said.

"Sure it did."

"But you said the robot agreed to let one person see it move." Jessy tilted her head to one side. "Right?"

"Right," Ben said. "I wanted it to be you."

She nodded. "I think maybe it was Stella instead."

Ben let out a long sigh. "That was still cheating," he said. "The robot talked in front of her before. Anyway, Stella doesn't count. She can't even talk."

Jessy laughed. "She can now," she said.

Stella was toddling around the kitchen. She had pulled spice jars out of the cupboard and was making towers with them. Mom was still on the phone.

"Stella," Ben said, "listen to me, okay? This is important."

"Ben." Stella smiled, pleased with her new skill.

"That's right. I'm Ben." He knelt down beside her. "You saw my robot, didn't you?"

"Wo boh go! Wo boh go!"

Ben nodded. "Out the front door, right? On roller skates?" He looked at her. "Ben's robot go, right?"

Stella laughed and knocked over her tower. "Ben wo boh go," she said firmly.

Ben stood up and turned to Jessy. "I guess I shouldn't have given it feet."

"Yeah, now you don't have a robot or roller skates."

"The skates were too small anyway," Ben said. *And the robot was too grumpy*, he thought to himself.

"I'm sorry about your robot," Jessy said softly.

"Yeah, it's okay. It never wanted to do anything anyway." Ben was a little sad that KX was gone. But in some ways, the robot had just caused problems. Besides, maybe KX would be happier somewhere else. And Jessy was a lot more fun to play with than any old robot. "Let's play Vikings," Ben said.

Jessy smiled. "Okay," she said.

57

They grabbed some capes and the construction helmets. Then they headed outside to Ben's backyard.

"Who are you going to be?" Jessy asked. She wrapped a cape over her shoulders and crammed the helmet on over her ponytail. "I want to be, um, Jessy the Red."

"I'll be Ben the Beastly," he said, grinning at her. Even without horns on her helmet, she really did look like a Viking. She looked ready for adventure. She looked ready to sail the seas.

Ben looked around the backyard. There was a pile of wood stacked by the fence. The wood scraps were for a tree house that Ben had never built. Ben eyed the wood thoughtfully. He felt an excited flutter in his tummy. "Jessy," he said, "let's build a *real* Viking ship."

Robin Stevenson is the author of a number of novels for older children and teens. *Ben's Robot* was inspired by Robin's five-year-old son, Kai, who asked for a story about a robot, and who, like Ben, collects all kinds of treasure and prefers his bread frozen. Robin lives in Victoria, British Columbia.